Pra

"This story is un ... t caregiving when someone you love is not going to get better, such as a dying parent." Kathy Dowdy

"If I had one word to describe this book, it would be HOPE." Janelle Blank

"This book is the perfect insight that not all special needs children are the same... You give your audience the 'real deal' when it comes to life and everyday issues." Zac

"What a powerful, moving story. Thank you for this loving gift." Linda Welsh

"The author shares his journey through an authentic, raw depiction of his life as a devoted father, husband, and caregiver." Angie Mills

"I became completely engrossed with each sitting... I found myself thinking about Savannah's story during the days, and even though it was painful to read, I looked forward to it every night. Thank you for being brave enough to share Savannah's story." Kim Goss

And Yet We Rise

And Yet We Rise

A Tale of Coping,
Overcoming,
and Transcending

David Borden

ScribbleFire
Austin

First Edition

Copyright 2017 by David Borden

All Rights Reserved

Some names and places have been changed. Some characters are composites of several people.

This edition may be cataloged as such:

1. Memoir. 2. Family Relationships. 3. Marriage. 4. Disability. 5. Parents of Children with Disabilities. 6. Loss. 7. Grief. 8. Caregiving 9. Graphic Novel

Published in the United States by

ScribbleFire

PO BOX 200512

Austin, TX 78720

www.scribblefire.com

This book is for Ruby and Savannah

"Bad things do happen; how I
respond to them defines my
character and the quality of my
life. I can choose to sit in perpetual
sadness, immobilized by the gravity
of my loss or I can choose
to rise
from the pain and treasure the
most precious gift I have—
life itself."
—Walter Anderson

Ruby

the truth is horrific and beautiful ...

Our story starts on March 5, 2015

Austin Fire Dept.

Police

This is the day that redefined our lives- again- this is the day your sister died weeks shy of her 16th birthday.

Your Mom called to me from Savannah's room as I prepared her cocktail of morning medicine

LAX o' LUX

Tamara's voice rang weirdly. I knew something was terribly wrong...

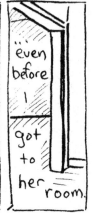

...even before I got to her room.

Savannah looked so peaceful. But I knew she wasn't sleeping. She had...

Dave, come here!

...that look of someone with no more use for this world.

I called **911**. The dispatcher told me to do **chest compressions**.

I put the phone on the floor. The dispatcher counted while I did CPR. It felt horrible forcing a dead person to breathe.

3

When EMS arrived, a supervisor took us to our kitchen - away from Savannah's room.

Do you have a **DNR***

No, We don't.

* Do Not Resuscitate

If you don't have a DNR, we have to work through our protocol. It will take 20 minutes.

But she's dead.

He had to look away. He'd seen this before.

I'm sorry. It's not a choice.

And you'll want to stay out of the room.

It took a gruelling 40 minutes. A neighbor saw EMS and brought us coffee. The grief counselors arrived. Savannah was declared dead.

The crime scene photographer took pictures of everything.

An officer in blue gloves counted every one of her pills to make sure we hadn't killed her.

We spent the first hour of our mourning being interrogated.

A cop hovered outside Savannah's door until the Medical Examiner released her body.

Tamara called our dear friends, Sarah and Chris, to come sit with us.

I'm so sorry.

If you need anything, just ask.

Their son and Savannah had been friends at school...

Here we go!

Until he died in his sleep a year and a half earlier.

click

I want to visit Mason.

click

Hello!

The police said we could visit her one last time before the funeral home picked her up.

We walked down the hall to her room

Tamara and I sat on the cold floor with her— where EMS had left her.

I don't want to remember her like this.

I left. I didn't want this image. She deserved better.

Tamara opened the curtains for the first time that morning

We hadn't realized that the sun had risen. It burst into the house, revealing a day full of clear blue sky and radiant sunshine, exactly like the day she was born.

Oh, Sara.

This is not a "clean" grief. It is filled with guilt because you miss this child you loved, but you're also relieved that her suffering and your burden of care has ended.

The grief counselor tried to talk to you, but you stayed quiet. You wanted to be strong.

You were only 11 years old, but you wrote this letter.

Dear Dad,
It's hard to think that I will never see my sister again. And I know it's even harder for you, but as your only daughter, now, I will do as much as I can to live up to Sister and make you smile like she made you smile. I know I'll never live up to her, but I'll at least try. So with all my heart I hope we can carry on, but I know it will never be the same without her. Ruby

I was so touched that I decided to write her back... but the words failed me.

ugh...

9

Dear Ruby,

Thank you for your letter. I'm sitting in your sister's room, trying to write you back. I'm here because I feel her presence lingering. I think she wants me to tell her story one more time, not for a doctor or social worker, but for us— our family— and people like us who are struggling with depression, mourning, feelings of isolation, the strain of caretaking, or that they can't live up to the expectations of others.

Although Savannah lived with tremendous pain and frustration, she pursued life with tenacity and humor. She overcame many obstacles and I'm so proud of her accomplishments. I've come to realize that her story— our story— is our most valuable possession. We must preserve it and share it. She showed us how to survive, and even thrive under the most difficult circumstances. She taught us how to bend instead of break, she taught us that when life is bleak, it is still possible to find the courage to rise.

Love, Dad

10

CHAPTER 1

Exploring the Negative Space

13

...and yet

I'd rise...

We took off work for two weeks. We told people: no phone calls, no emails, no visits,

Friends brought food so we'd remember to eat

I forgot to water the plants.

The cat kept checking Savannah's room

Meow?

to see if she'd returned.

15

We binged on comic books, popcorn, and pizza. We snuggled and watched Savannah's TV.

CHAPTER

2

The
Path to the
Beach is
Uphill

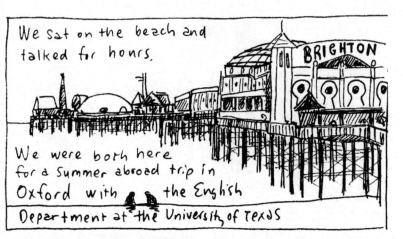

We sat on the beach and talked for hours.

We were both here for a summer abroad trip in Oxford with the English Department at the University of Texas

I sketched the pier while we talked

We hung out all the time

I should tell you that I have a girl-friend back home.

That's okay, we can just be friends

A few days later, I received a three page letter in tight, scratchy pen from my girlfriend. She'd met someone else.

I'd always relished a letter from a girl- fun, flirty, and warm, but this one felt like a kick in the stomach.

I panicked. I'd lost a girlfriend and if I didn't do anything, now, I'd lose Tamara, too. The words from our last conversation rang in my head.

I can't do this.

By now, the paper had lost its crinkle. It felt horrible, but I had to share it. She'd become my best friend.

We have a photo of us in the old quad at Brasenose College, Oxford on the last night of the trip. We look so young, so innocent.

We're all dressed up. Tamara- porcelain-skinned and blushing with happiness.

My golden hair flows over my strong shoulders.

That winter, we applied to graduate schools. Tamara's rabbit nibbled at our packets and we spilled wine on our return postcards. We were somber - figuring we'd go to different schools and, therefore, break up.

Hey, Little Fella.

OXFORD

That Spring Tamara said:

What do you know about Guam?

It's an island in the Pacific,

It's tropical

They eat bats.

Why?

My brother's girlfriend's mother teaches English there at a community college

Cel's a beer!

We stayed up until 3am. to call because of the time difference.

How do we get jobs like that?

You need a Master's degree

Come with me to Denton! UNT and move overseas.

We'll get Master's at

Maybe an island?

Maybe France?

red wine.

Clear blue skies and sandy beaches.

adventure

Sold!

After graduation, we landed jobs in Morocco.

We sold most everything and packed the remainder in two suitcases,

We taught English in Rabat for two years before moving to Agadir to run a school for three more.

It was an exciting time.

We vacationed in Spain, Portugal, and Britain. Our friends envied our life style and our thrilling adventures.

Our lives were perfect—careers, relationship, travel. We decided to complement it all by adding a perfect child. She'd go to the best schools, travel the world with us, and become an important artist or scientist...

... what could possibly go wrong with this plan?

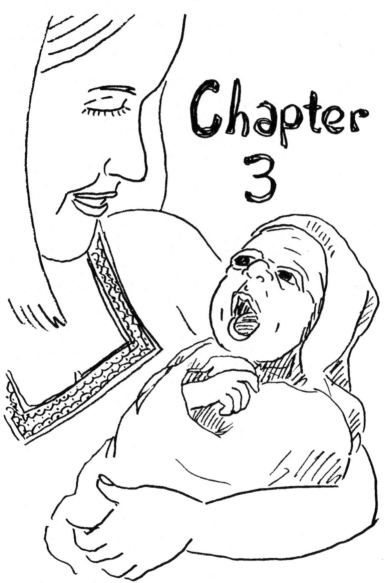

Chapter
3

April Fool's Day, 1999

Sunshine on a sparkling ocean

Cool breeze

rustling leaves

lazy afternoon

Resting on an indigo blanket

as if floating on a calm sea before the storm

pop!

Did you hear that?

We're going to have a baby.

Tamara stood in the cool, spring air, rubbing her abdomen. I wish to savor this moment, so full of joy and potential happiness. What if I could stop the story right here — shoot it off in a better direction? If I had done one thing differently, would the outcome have been better?

Did you get my bags?

Yes!

Did you lock the door?

Close your eyes— I'm entering the round-a-bout

The Talborjt neighborhood flew past in a blur. The white-washed buildings sprouting rebar, carpets airing, bright awnings, and people bustling.

16

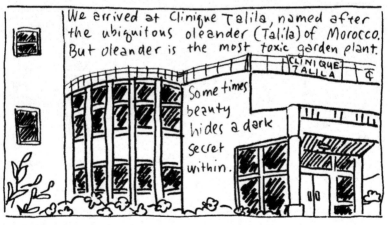

Le bébe est trop lent.

Though I didn't understand every word the doctor said the meaning was clear.

Nous avons besoin pour l'aider

Savannah came into this world with the umbilical cord around her throat.

Is it a boy or girl?

I don't know. She took it away too fast.

Why isn't it crying?

Infirmière, venir ici rapidment

C'est une fille.

It's a girl!

It's a girl! It's a girl!

And we were happy for an instant.

The next morning

Madame, comment s'est passé votre nuit?

She didn't really sleep last night, and she didn't eat at all.

Nous la prenons et la nourrir.

Okay

It's been a long time. Don't you think we ought to check on her?

Let's walk down to the nursery.

Slowly please, I'm still in a lot of pain.

Okay

Savannah! What's happening?

Elle a eu une crise

A what? I don't understand, "une crise?"

Heh, en Anglais? une "Seizure."

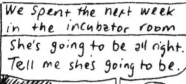

We spent the next week in the incubator room

She's going to be all right. Tell me she's going to be.

Nurse Fatima would detach all the wires and help Tamara try to feed her.

No! That hurts!

You look raw, Do you want to rest?

One more time. I need her to eat.

Are you sure?

I have to feed my baby— She has to eat!

Take her. It's going to be okay.

No, it's not, I'm a failure as a mom.

Madame?

Nurse Fatima returned Savannah to the incubator, inserted a feeding tube up her nose, and attached a pulse-oxygen monitor to her toe.

It felt like a defeat.

On the second day, a man peered into the room through the tiny, door window. He looked dazed. Nurse Fatima said that his wife had had pre-mature labor with twins. The first baby died, then the wife died. They saved the second baby, but it needed an incubator — and Savannah had the only one at the clinic.

He stalked the hallways and frequently checked to see if our child survived — if we still needed the incubator.

I dont know what became of him and his dying baby

I still think of that man, wandering the empty halls like a phantom, I wonder how our lives would have unfolded if, instead, Savannah had died under that clear, blue sky, with gleaming talilas all around. I'm sure we would have cursed the universe for its cruelty, its indifference, and its unfairness.

Perhaps we would have continued to travel the world, but would that adventure have been as rich, as profound, as the one in which we had already embarked?

Sixteen Tons and What do You Get ?

Chapter

4

45

chapter 5

THE HOUSE of UNMET EXPECTATIONS

Feedings went like this: She'd refuse

and cry and cry and cry until

she screamed for 20 minutes at a high note

She'd latch poorly, dribble most of it out, and slowly eat for 45 minutes

She had as much milk on her as in her.

Suddenly, she'd writhe and squirm.

Do you need to burp?

Gack

Gug.

Damn-it.

BLECH!

I'd clean her up...

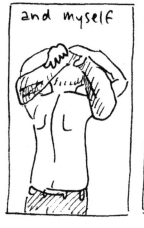

and myself

and start over. It's no wonder she wasn't gaining weight

49

When we weren't taking care of Savannah, we were looking for jobs.

WAH!

Every Thursday, my parents arrived late, carrying food. They wanted to relax, but Savannah wouldn't let them.

wah!

The house was never as clean as they wanted it.

Your father and I are going to bed. I wish you wouldn't feed her on my good sofa.

Since you don't seem to know how to clean a bathroom, I'll show you.

Mom, I'm 30 years old. And I just cleaned it.

Our presence caused a lot of stress.

51

We made an appointment with a family doctor near Lakeway. We didn't have health insurance; however, we'd saved money for a few appointments before we could find jobs.

Is it supposed to be this hard?

Everyone says the first year is difficult.

Not this difficult! If babies were this hard, people would stop having them.

You're right. They're not supposed to be like this.

Can you get another bib? This one's already soaked.

I'm afraid something's not right.

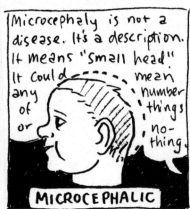

54

I'm scared.

Me, too.

While waiting for the appointment with the specialist, I got a job as a part-time English teacher.

My name is David

I'll be your teacher

Ironically, the entire class were Moroccans

Teacher, did Morocco surprise you?

Yes, I expected Sahara, but it wasn't like that at all.

Let's talk about the word: "expect." Is Texas what you expected?

No. It's not like TV.

No wild animals or cowboys or desert

expect

None of this is what I expected.

expect

expectation

Chapter 6

Take Her Home and Love Her

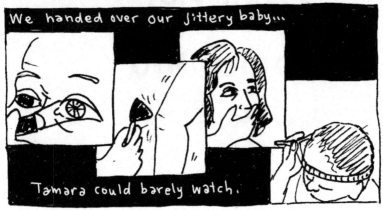

We were so exhausted. We didn't want platitudes or blind optimism. We didn't want abstractions. We wanted a guide. We wanted practical advice on how to feed this child who refused to eat. We wanted to know how to soothe this child who cried for hours—days at a time — who didn't sleep. We wanted to quiet her seizures. Instead he gave us much more: our guiding principle.

Just take her home and love her.

Chapter
7

Judgment

Something's wrong. I think we should talk about what's bothering you.

The stress of the baby and our cohabitation had been building up.

Wah!

My mother's blood pressure had gone up and she was agitated. Her face tired and lined - her hair uncharacteristically out of place.

We work so hard... and we're so tired. What do you want us to do around the house that we're not doing now?

Oh, nothing... It's just groceries get expensive.

We can buy groceries.

You wasted all that time... five worthless years you wasted. Your experience overseas amounts to nothing. No one wants to hire you. I'd never hire you for a job. When you've been hiring and firing as long as I have. You'll understand.

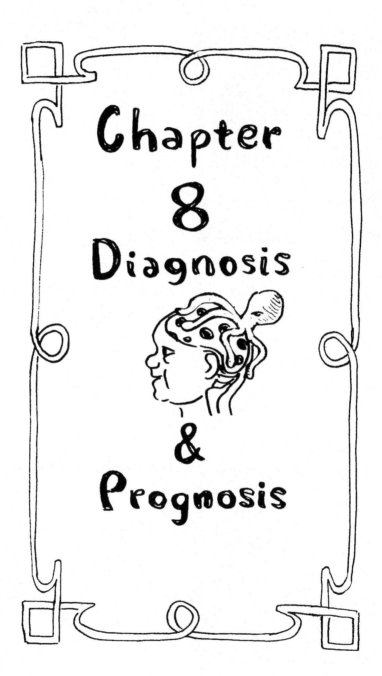

Chapter
8
Diagnosis
&
Prognosis

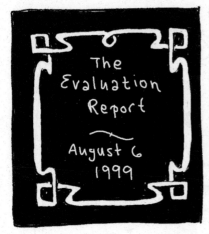

The
Evaluation
Report

August 6
1999

Did **you** have a chance to read Savannah's Evaluation Report from the hospital?

Ugh... not yet.

Blah, blah, blah, percent this... percent that, ugh, this is so depressing. The last line on page 3 reads:

"Team Summary! Final diagnostic category is abnormal."

What a label to slap on a child so early in life.

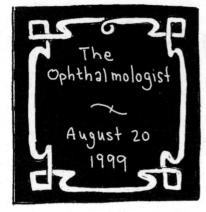

The
Ophthalmologist

August 20
1999

She is legally blind.

The eyes work fine. The problem is brain damage. So much is destroyed that the signal gets lost and garbled on its long journey to the optic center

So, what can she see?

Everything and nothing. The world looks like wallpaper to her. She can't distinguish shapes from one another. It is confusing and overwhelming.

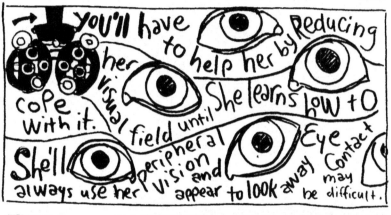

You'll have to help her by Reducing her visual field until she learns how to cope with it. She'll always use her peripheral vision and appear to look away. Eye contact may be difficult.

Labor Day, 1999

~

We moved to a small rent house in South Austin

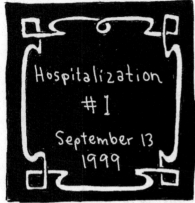

Hospitalization
#1
September 13
1999

Do you have to glue those things on? It seems so medieval.

It's fine. It comes off with solvent.

How do you know it's fine? I bet you've never had it done to you.

Of course not.

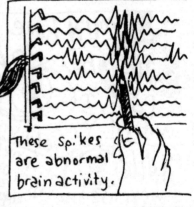

These spikes are abnormal brain activity.

Seizures...

All we can do is give her some medications and wait and watch.

wah!

Shh. It's okay

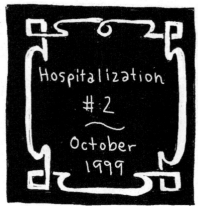

Hospitalization
#2
~
October
1999

Another EEG

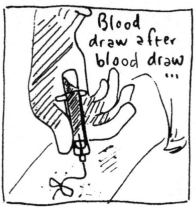

Blood draw after blood draw ...

New drug after new drug...

The drugs caused violent reactions. She was terrified. All the adults she meet brought her pain..

Days passed

whah!

wah

wah!

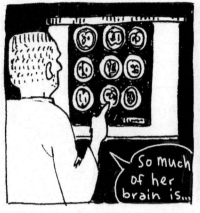

So much of her brain is...

...damaged that I can do nothing for you here in Austin. You'll have to go to Houston.

I wish I could go, too.

I'm such a bad mother.

Don't say that. We're doing what we have to do.

Wah!

Remember the deal? You got a job with health insurance, so you work— I'll take care of Savannah.

We'll survive some how.

Wah!

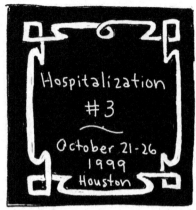

Hospitalization
#3

October 21-26
1999
Houston

Beep... Beep... Beep...

More tests... more drugs more blood more vomit more sleeplessness.

Best we can tell: Oxygen was cut off to her brain around the time of her birth. A stroke- a brain injury- its all the same now

I took to wandering the halls while she slept- like the phantom of Agadir.

Because she's not responding to any treatments, we're scheduling exploratory brain surgery.

72

The House
of the
Martian Year

Chapter 9

...annah was six months old. And because she was sensitive to light, we kept the blinds shut.

The air conditioner railed against the flimsy insulation.

This is our 800 square foot prison on Mars:

A desert of time, where a baby cries all night and refuses to eat, seizes and projectile vomits after every painful meal.

wah!

Mars orbits so far from the sun that it is no longer a companion, but a lonely object in the blackness of space. A year lasts extra long: 686.9 Earth days.

ss!

Houston, we have a problem, over. I'm stranded with no way to get home, over.

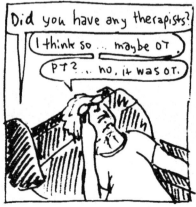

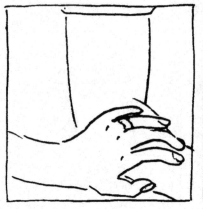

How was your day?

Busy.

First, I had to... and then... next... and you won't believe what happened when...

What's the matter?

Hearing you talk about wok is like listening to a girl you've got a crush on talking about how much she loves her boyfriend.

Oh! It wasn't OT or PT. she had vision therapy today. I knew I'd remember!

83

Chapter 10
Why does David Look Like a Junkie?

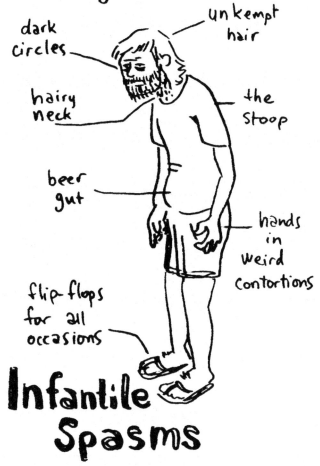

dark circles

unkempt hair

hairy neck

the stoop

beer gut

hands in weird contortions

flip-flops for all occasions

Infantile Spasms

With her neurologist's help, I finally found a pharmacy that would sell me the syringes.

Let's begin treatment:

① Warm up the cold, viscous medicine so that you can inject it less painfully.

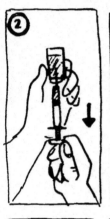

②

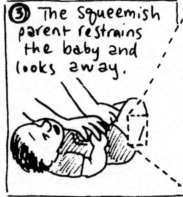

③ The squeemish parent restrains the baby and looks away.

④

⑤ Jab quickly or it bounces off

⑥ She cries as you push the medicine in slowly

⑦ Count to ten while you push...

1 Mississippi
2 Mississippi
3 Mi
4 M
5 M
6 M

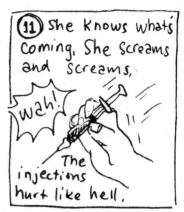

13. The Infantile Spasms abate after many weeks.

"She seems better."

I'm exhausted, but it feels good to finally have a victory.

14. "I don't recognize you"

This stranger has been initiated into a strange world.

He's the kind of guy who can inflict pain on a baby for its own good.

15. This guy placates himself with talk.

The ends justify the means

because he knows it will get worse before it gets better.

Chapter 11

The House of Endless Chores

I hired the cheapest carpenter I could find...

You see dat, bro? Dat's termites. Day gone, but dat beam's gone, too.

$

You see this bus ber? Melted. The whole box has to be replaced.

$100

I pulled up some nasty floor tile I found under the carpet.

My dad came by to help!

You know that tile is probably made of asbestos.

It's just vinyl.

Asbestos never hurt no one, 'cept maybe if a roll fell on someone's head and crushed him. It's all a lie made up by the liberal media.

I'm ignoring you.

By the way, did you notice that a lot of coloreds live in your neighborhood?

I'm ignoring you and your 1950's language.

We split Savannah duty on the weekends. I'd take one whole day...

wah! wah!

...and Tamara would take the next.

ssshhh wah!

This isn't working. You'll need to be more specific: our life? The schedule? Us?

All of the above

Something has to give. I keep thinking we'll catch a break, but we don't.

We'll catch a break when she dies.

Don't say that. It isn't funny.

It's not funny; you aren't funny any more.

That's because it's hard to be funny when everything is so depressing. Plus, I'm stuck with her all week. She drains me of everything.

But I have to work. It's very stressful. What if I lost this job? I can't lose this job, We're one paycheck away from being homeless.

I come home tired. The house is always a mess. Why don't you clean it while you're here? I dread weekends — I get no rest. All I do is work, clean, and take care of Savannah,

I'm going to bed.

huh?

The distance between us grew larger,

I can't do this any more.

Hang in there. A couple of more weeks and she'll be eligible for Open Door

I hate being home with her. I thought I could do this but I can't, I hate this life more than anything. I'm not cut out for caretaking.

You'll be fine. You're a strong man - a strong, caring man - and I love you for it.

I never wanted children in the first place.

So, what you're saying is this is all my fault?

...

Nice...

April 1, 2001 I celebrated Savannah's second birthday by taking her to...

...pre-school at Open Door. At the time, it was the only day care

OPEN DOOR Pre-school

in Austin that would take a significantly disabled child.

I spent two weeks training the staff.

No, don't give up yet. She's about to latch on.

Its too bright and noisy out here. You have to take her to a quiet, dark room to eat.

That one, over there, looks perfect.

Savannah loved being with the other kids.

On the first day, I could leave her a few hours I rolled down the windows and blasted the radio.

I can't get no — NO, NO, NO...

I was so weary and happy for a morsel of freedom that I cried.

That afternoon, I took a nap... and slept like a man who believed that one day he could be resurrected.

Chapter 12

Is this the End of the World?

My brother called. He was stranded in Boston. He couldn't get through to his wife. Their apartment was so close to the towers that the dust from collapse ruined people's homes.

Tamara called.

Hey, everything's fine here. Savannah's at Open Door.

Are you crazy? Don't you see what's happening?

LIVE

I guess I should pick her up.

Ya think?

Ok. I'll get her after I shower and nap.

Shit.

It looked like the world was coming to an end...

I wept... but did I weep for the thousands who died in front of our eyes? Or did I weep because this tragedy set off a flood of pain and sorrow trapped inside of me?

I drove back to Open Door—few staff and children remained.

"If this is the apocalypse," I said to Savannah, "I'll take care of you until the end... and we'll go together into the abyss."

Chapter 13

That's Mr. Dad to You!

Do you need me to show you again? No.

Will you do it my way?

Yes

I'm glad we understand each other.

Tamara quickly learned that we could play good cop/bad cop with doctors, teachers, therapists...

Would you rather speak to Dave? I didn't think so.

No. That's a terrible - even stupid idea...

But it's my professional opinion -

Let's make a deal.

Tamara's power grew. She became a supreme negotiator.

Excellent. I knew you'd see it our way.

What happened?

A few years later, we knew we had taken it too far when I was called to pick up Savannah and the school principal was waiting with the classroom teacher in order to "avoid an incident."

We're all friends now, and laugh about it, but it wasn't funny at the time.

And, going out in public always produced some awkward situations...

How old is your infant?

Three.

Oh.. um.. er.. I'm...

Is your baby sleeping?

I'm a monster!

No, she's blind.

Oh...er, I'm... sorry.

grrrr.

Mommy, Mommy, what's that baby doing?

Having a seizure.

Don't stare. Come along.

gack.

I learned not to care what people thought or whether they stared. I loved her for who she was.

We left amid people talking and laughing.

Wah!

Did you see the child Savannah's age feeding herself?

Yes, it made me sad.

Wah!

All I ever wanted was a healthy baby... and those people don't even know how lucky they are. They don't appreciate a "normal" child. Why do they get that, and I don't?

By the time we got home, Savannah calmed.

I'll put on a video.

We sat at our crooked table and ate from Styrofoam — our "big night out."

I just wanted to drink too much beer.

Tamara had hit rock bottom. That night she'd had enough and started planning her path out of her hole. I had still a couple of years to go.

Chapter 15

Planned

Optimism

114

A few days later.

Have you thought about it?

Give me a proposal — a business plan. I want to know how it will work.

At first, she thought I was kidding, but when she realized I wasn't, she wrote something up.

She made arrangements for Savannah to stay with my parents. She booked a "retreat" for us at a quiet B&B in the Texas Hill Country.

We sat on the porch drinking beer while I read her plan.

I've been thinking...

What if Savannah lives a long time? Who'll look out for her? Who'll check on her, advocate for her when we can't?

We rocked on the porch while the sun slowly sank. I thought about my assertion that love divides with the addition of new people. Actually, love grows in response to the need.

Lavender bushes bloomed on the porch.

How optimistic the little flowers seemed continuing to bloom, sharing their beauty with the world.

Chapter 16

A Starvation
Diet

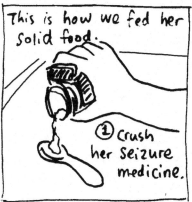

119

③ Here you go. Take your meds.

④ Because of her cerebral palsy, she spits out more than she swallows

⑤ Don't punch me in the face. I'm trying to help you.

⑥ I've got you. No choking.

⑦ Frequently, she gags. Swallow.

⑧ Often, she vomits it all back up.

crap!

⑨ Okay. Let's continue.

⑩ Here's a drink.

⑪ My back's getting tired.

⑫ We've been at this an hour. Are you tired, too?

⑬ Have I become a ghost?

(14) Shhh. It's okay, Sweetie, come back to me.

(15) What kind of life is this? How long will we survive?

Let me wipe your face.

When she recovered, she blinked. She looked straight at me. There was no recognition.

We're a pair, aren't we? Where do you end and where do I begin? Where has my life gone and where is it going?

Come on. We're finished. Let's get cleaned up.

Maybe we'll have better luck tomorrow.

122

At the doctor's office

Her weight is dangerously low. It's time to consider a feeding tube.

We just need a little more time. We can do this.

Savannah screamed with hunger, but would not eat. She spat and punched me in the face at every meal.

I shoved food into her as best I could. It was hard to watch a child slowly starve.

Sixteen tons and what...

To keep her alive I bottle fed her, too

No one believed I spent 8-10 hours a day feeding her

Sometimes I didn't believe it myself.

How many boxes did you check? ____
Perhaps he should visit his doctor...

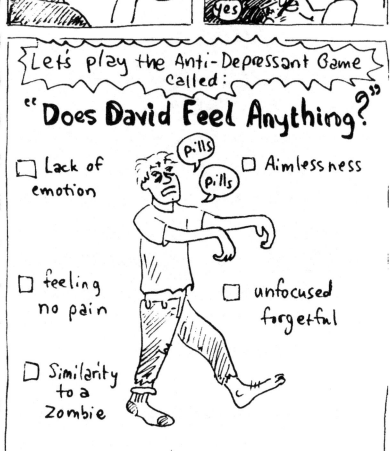

Chapter 17

Enter

Not an Exit

Warning:
Labyrinth Ahead

In Austin, all pediatric neurology was under one monopoly umbrella.

It's our way or no way.

Have a nice day.

Pediatric Neurology has a dispute with our insurance company, so we'll have to self-pay or drive to San Antonio until its resolved.

What?

I told our ophthalmologist about our neuro problem.

I guess we have to go to San Antonio.

Austin Neuro is notorious.

I have a friend who used to practice pedi-neuro, I'll talk to him, I bet he'll make an exception to see Savannah.

Now, hold her still while I dialate her eyes.

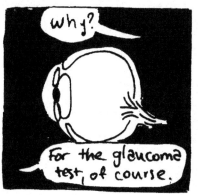
Why?

For the glaucoma test, of course.

She takes Seize-o-max, doesn't she?

Yes.

Pressure

Didn't her neuro tell you that glaucoma is a risk factor?

No.

In spite of that side effect, the pharma company wants to market Seize-o-Max as a diet pill?

Why?

Because it's a strong appetite suppressant.

No way! That explains a lot. I'm fighting oral aversions, cerebral palsy, and Seize-o-max!

Oh, my God. You didn't know this?

But what's worse - because the market for diet pills is so large, they want to mass market the drug even though it has this glaucoma risk.

Personally I think its better to be fat than blind.

The New Neurologist.

I don't see children anymore. I'll see her until this insurance business is sorted out.

I see she's on Seize-o-Max. I'll put her on a potassium supplement. Didn't you know Seize-o-Max leaches potassium?

He was gruff...

...but...

...he knew his stuff.

Can we continue seeing you? Pediatric Neurology Corporation of Austin is not meeting our needs.

I'm sorry.

I get this request all the time. If I took everyone with a complaint about PNCA, I'd be overwhelmed. I'm retiring soon. I wish I could help, but I can't. I wish you the best of luck.

A few weeks later...

PNCA has settled with our insurance. We can return.

Damn. The other doctor was better.

Back to our semi-annual neuro appointment...

Out of order

CAUTION CAUTION CAUTION

level 3 parking

I had to carry her down 3 flights of stairs to her appointment.

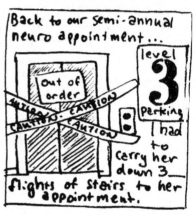

When we arrived at PNCA, the door was locked. A note was taped to the door.

PNCA

What the hell?

Pediatric Corp of Austin has moved to a new location. See map!

MAP

Come on, Savannah, we're going to be late.

We walked through the hospital basement to get to the new office

We passed strange machines, odd waiting areas and lonely places that time forgot

Savannah giggled at the galloping pace.

giggle

ALL Patients MUST check-in

Welcome to PNCA

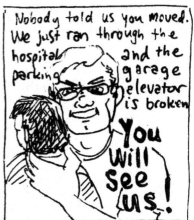

132

The Sunday Cooking Show

Chapter 18

Sunday 2005: Every week, we made baby food for Savannah.

At six years old, Savannah only weighed 24 pounds.

We made the fattiest, highest calorie

¡super loca! enchalada

baby food possible.

I hated this work. It reminded me that this child who should be in first grade has to be hand fed baby food.

I poured pears into the food mill. I used to love the smell of pears, but now they reek of dread.

I tried to use the blender, which was so much easier, but Savannah choked on the coarse food and seized at the sound of it.

The mill grinds the food more smoothly and quietly. However, it is laborious and makes me tired.

Sometimes the mill slips and spills every where.

Damn-it!

Tamara is there to help

Have another beer.

This work requires strength, stamina, and time.

Take a break, Pace yourself.

No. I want to be finished.

Grinding vegetables...

and entrees!

We used to be idealistic. A year earlier, we'd never have considered installing a

Mic-key Button

in order to...

...feed her through a tube...

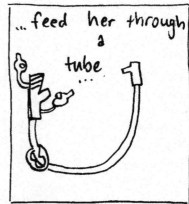

...into a hole in the wall of her stomach.

I scooped the baby food into blue plastic trays, covered them in plastic wrap, and slid them into the

freezer.

Some of her therapists worried that if we tubed her, the lack of oral stimulation would slow her already slow development.

GUILT

We worried that we'd deduct a sensory experience from a child already blind, mute, and physically challenged.

Chapter 19
Attendant Care

In 2008, Savannah's name came up on a waiting list for attendant care.

Excellent. The attendant can start tomorrow. Wonderful.

But attendants quit before finishing training

Why didn't Lupe show up for work today?

Oh

So she won't be back?

Crap.

After Ruby's birth, I started working more at the college. When care fell through, I scrambled to cover.

I have to go.

But what about my TPS reports?

Dealing with Savannah's issues, her intense care, full-time jobs, and a toddler, wore on us.

Mommy Mommy Mom

Wah!

Then our savior arrived

Hello.

Hi, I'm from the service.

My name is Diamond.

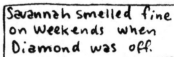

141

143

Diamond, why is there vomit on the sofa cushion?

There weren't. I cleaned it up.

But you didn't. That's how we found it.

I cleaned it up. I always do.

What do you mean, "always?"

When I need to run errands, I take my sweet 'Vanna with me. She likes getting out of the house.

How you doin' back there, 'Vanna?

But you don't have a car seat?

Don't need one. I wedge her in between two of the sofa cushions.

Oh my God! That's not legal or safe and you aren't authorized and we haven't given permission.

144

We were in a bind. Diamond was reliable.

Savannah and Ruby liked her a lot.

If we fired Diamond, we'd have to leave work early to meet the bus.

We could overlook her long phone conversations with family and friends.

We could overlook the fact that she left food crumbs on the sofa and toenail clippings on the coffee table.

But we drew the line at Savannah's safety. We fired her and our lives once again plunged into chaos...

Chapter
20

Cheers!

147

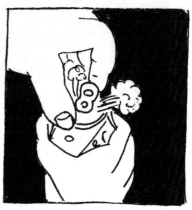

149

Chapter 21

THE NIGHT IS LONG

Her cry wound up like an old-fashioned, hand-cranked air raid siren

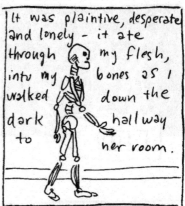

It was plaintive, desperate and lonely - it ate through my flesh, into my bones as I walked down the dark to her room.

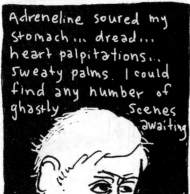

Adreneline soured my stomach... dread... heart palpitations... sweaty palms. I could find any number of ghastly scenes awaiting

Night duty belonged to me.

Savannah, what's going on?

I don't feel any fever. Does something hurt?

At 3 a.m., her deep brown eyes plead, "Help me, Daddy."

Did you have a bad dream? Daddy's here.

moan

She's wet with sweat and drool and fear.

153

A helicopter thumped through the night

a racoon ran across the roof...

Shh. Let's walk around. I'll sing to you.

It occurred to me that my soul felt chafed and irritated under my skin.

It's dark as a dungeon way down in the mine. ♫

My insides had rotted into a heap of junk.

It will form as a habit— seep into your soul. ♫

I was sinking like this house with its broken foundation— sinking into the 3 a.m. dark

Savannah? It's okay. It's just a seizure.

Maybe the best way to alleviate her pain is to end it right here?

But I could never do it. I could never murder my own child. I love her too much.

Maybe I should kill myself instead? Now, that's the best idea I've had in a long time! I could crawl into the arms of the void and Sleep...

The amazing thing about hitting rock bottom is this: when you're there, it's not apparent...

So, this is the abyss.

I didn't know I'd reached the bottom because the hole felt infinite in depth

What is the difference between people who manage to hang on by their fingertips and those who succumb to the temptation to let go? The temptation is strong and real and Sweet.

It wasn't until later, when I could look down from the surface that I could see where I'd caught hold.

157

Maybe We Can Do This

A bonus chapter made possible
by my generous backers
on Kickstarter

159

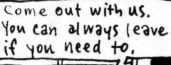

Come out with us. You can always leave if you need to.

okay.

Hey, can I talk to you for a minute?

Amy and Sean want us to have a few beers with them at Central Market park.

That would've been fun. You told them "no," right?

Hey, there they are!

All's well so far.

Tamara, I'm so glad you made it.

Me too.

Beer?

Ruby played on the playscape. Savannah sat calmly, she watched and listened.

Ha! Ha! Ha! Ha! Ha! Ha!

Chapter 22

Two
Wrongs Make
a Right

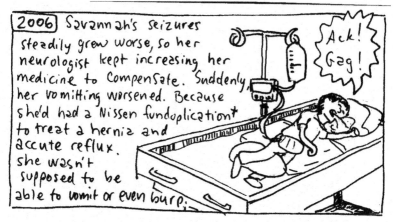

2006 | Savannah's seizures steadily grew worse, so her neurologist kept increasing her medicine to compensate. Suddenly, her vomiting worsened. Because she'd had a Nissen fundoplication* to treat a hernia and accute reflux, she wasn't supposed to be able to vomit or even burp.

Ack! Gag!

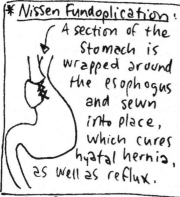

*Nissen Fundoplication: A section of the stomach is wrapped around the esophogus and sewn into place, which cures hyatal hernia, as well as reflux.

*GI: Gastro-Intestinal

It creates a one-way valve, rendering it difficult to retch. The poor child appeared to be gripped with excruciating pain every time she heaved.

I wish I could help.

Doctor, she's crying and throwing up constantly. She's stopped sleeping. She's exhausted and hungry and very sick.

Take her to her GI surgeon* immediately.

At the GI surgeon's office

I've never seen anything like this! Go to the hospital immediately. I'll call and tell them to admit her.

ACK! WAH! GAG!

Checking-in at the hospital took a long time.

But Dr. Gutt sent us here, she needs immediate attention.

I'm sorry, sir. I'll call again.

WAH!

Admissions

Eventually, we got a room.

Can you get her something for pain?

If I were to write a TV Hospital Drama, it would be much different from the fast-paced action you see. I'd show the TRUTH:

Nothing would happen for hours at a time. Dialogue would consist of apologies and excuses...

I'm sorry. I can't do anything until Dr. McDreamy answers my page

DAY 1 Around 3am., after constant badgering from me and the nurse, a resident ordered a pain-killer. We both slept for the first time in days.

ZZZ

Promptly at 5am, Nurse Reveille jabbed a thermometer in Savannah and revved up the blood pressure cuff. The tranquility was broken.

WAH! WAH!

167

DAY 2 | She writhed until she was sweaty. She sweated until she was dehydrated. She cried until her lips split open and bled. She heaved. We could do nothing but watch her decline.

We can't figure out what's wrong, so we've scheduled some exploratory surgery for tomorrow.

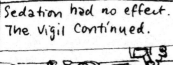

Sedation had no effect. The vigil continued.

wah. ack.

I'm going to pick up some dinner and Ruby. Be back soon.

How was your day, Ruby?

Good. Is Sister okay?

No, but she'll be okay.

See you tomorrow.

Bye, Mommy.

I love you.

It was Tamara's turn to spend the night.

DAY 3 Hey, Sweetie, you look so much better.

She even slept last night.

Without surgery? Awesome!

This morning a different neurologist stopped by. She said:

Savannah's seizure medication levels were high enough to even make an adult sick. Her cure is ironic.

SEIZE AWAY MAGIC ELIXER

The hospital recorded her medication dosage wrong at intake, so they've been grossly "under dosing" her since she arrived.

What does that have to do with her GI problem?

There wasn't a GI problem! Never was. Her neuro over-dosed her on Seize Away. She was poisoned.

She's cured because the hospital's mistake fixed the doctor's mistake?

Yep.

One mistake fixed the other.

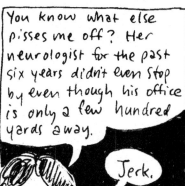

You know what else pisses me off? Her neurologist for the past six years didn't even stop by even though his office is only a few hundred yards away.

Jerk.

169

→ The Next Day ⇄

We have no sense of humor, sir. If you'd like a different neurologist, I suggest you find one in San Antonio.

What?

I said, "you can go to San Antonio.

oh.

For a moment I thought I heard you say, "you can go to hell."

The **Ketogenic Diet** is a real treatment for children with seizures (uncontrolled by medicine.). It is effective in half of those who undertake it. This chapter is NOT a criticism or denunciation of the treatment, which has helped many people.

Savannah was not a good candidate for the diet, but her nutritionist had an agenda. She felt the diet was better than medicine — no discussion.

The world of chronic illness and disability is full of zealots who peddle their pet ideas on parents and loved ones. The following

Tale of The Snake Oil Sales Person

aims to represent the broad class of charlatans and opportunists and bullies we encountered.

Step right up, my Dear Unfortunates! Partake of the **CURE.** Simple and easy. Relief is in your grasp. In fact, if you don't try it, you're delinquent parents with a disease of the soul.

I declare. Tell me what to do! I want to be a good mother.

Just follow these easy steps to a utopian future!

Q: what's the size of a silver dollar?

Q: Surgically implanted under the skin?

Q: has a wire that runs up the neck, coiling around the vagus nerve?

Q: pulses electric current to disrupt seizure activity?

Q: Can be described as a pace-maker for epilepsy?

Chapter 24

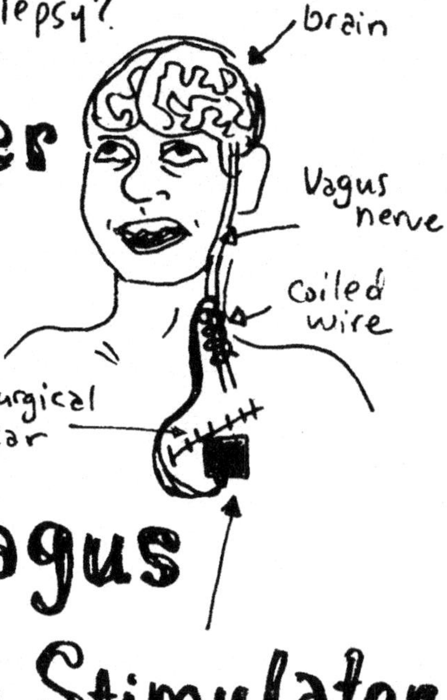

A:

The Vagus Nerve Stimulator

brain

Vagus nerve

Coiled wire

surgical scar

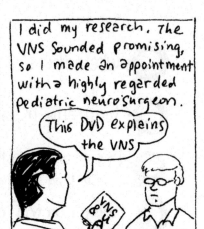

Chapter 25

THE ENORMOUS GREEN BINDER

Savannah Borden

2008 | Savannah's name came up on the waiting list for nursing care after eight years. We had a terrible time finding a nurse who only wanted an after school to bed shift.

"I'd like to help, but I need more hours."

We need another nurse.

"Tamara, I like you a lot. I want to send you a good nurse, but in the meantime I need to send you Nurse BM"

"What's wrong with her?"

"Oh, did I imply she was bad? No, no, no, she's just ...um... odd."

"That's fine. We're odd, ourselves."

"I want you to know - this is only temporary."

Nurse BM ran off other nurses we tried.

"You're not keeping the notes right in the binder."

"You're crazy. I'm outta here."

Nurse BM was, indeed, odd, but she showed up for work... and most importantly, Savannah liked her.

"Nice day, isn't it, Ya-ya?"

Things went well for a while.

"Time to eat, Ya-ya"

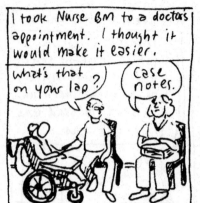

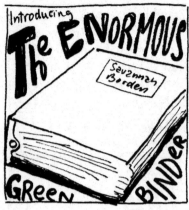

The BROWN RECLUSE is a seldom seen Texas native who likes to hide in shoes, the backs of closets, and places you'd rather not put your hand. The bite produces necrosis of the skin, which is horrible and unmistakable. Sometimes large sections of flesh must be surgically removed to prevent the onset of gangrene.

If this bite's two days old, there's no way it's a Brown Recluse. Just put an over-the-counter ointment on it,

But anti-biotics kill intestinal flora. Can you give me a prescription for a pro-biotic?

I said, use a TOPICAL ointment.

You never know. It's good to have it, just in case.

You can use an over-the-counter probiotic.

I need that in writing.

Is there anything else?

I only came in to get some papers signed. Honest.

We need a prescription for Glycopyrol to dry up her oral secretions— prevent choking

Shut up BM. Shut up... We don't need any of this... Just shut up... shut up...

Maybe choking is a bit strong. She struggles with saliva.

Excuse me, Doctor, but we need you out here for a minute.

After the doctor left, Nurse BM shut up.

oh, my, God. That must be important. They never take a doctor out of a room unless its a situation I know I used to work in an office like this..

"The Soliloquy of Nurse B.M."

Well, if Glycopyrol doesn't work, the next step will be Botox injections and if that doesn't work, we'll have to go to a tracheotomy. Those are the steps. I had a patient once who choked on secretions so we had no choice, we had to get a...

Through it all...

...she clung to the

lunatic

Enormous Green Binder

Chapter 26
The Adventures of Nurse B.M.

Baron Munchausen - is a fictional character, famous for his impossible exploits that include flying to the moon and riding a canon ball.

Munchausen By Proxy - is a psychological disorder in which a caregiver creates ficticious ailments in order to get sympathy or attention.

In 2008 we moved to a new house — The House of the Christmas Lights. I got a promotion at work and Savannah had the most challenging year ever.

She had grown into a gnarled branch, like the trees of Central Texas. Her spine continued to curve, her hip dislocated, and her knees floated, sometimes popping into painful positions.

Luckily, Nurse BM was there to help...

WAH!

...or so we thought. The dislocation came only when 'Nurse BM' was on duty.

WAH!

I grew suspicious.

It's happened again. Don't worry; I'll take care of it.

WAH!

Poor girl didn't pee last night. That's two days.

Yeah, this bottle is nearly empty.

whimper

shake shake

It all adds up: The blow out diarrhea, the lack of urine, BM's been secretly dosing her. The child's intestines must be in knots! She's dehydrated. No wonder she feels so bad.

The agency called and said BM told them Savannah's health's failing and she needs more hours.

I told her doctor that I suspected Munchausen by Proxy, but she said it was unlikely. People need to get something out of it.

Hours

Bingo

She's poisoning Savannah to get more hours.

Mommy's going to turn on the TV for you.

Without Nurse BM around, Savannah was back to normal by Sunday — for our weekly sing-a-long...

♫ but the cat came back...

Aye-ga-ga

We tried to replace Nurse BM without success.

I can't work this schedule.

I don't work with children

I don't show up for my shift.

Unable to prove Nurse BM was hurting Savannah, and unable to find a replacement, I locked away all the medicines and doled out daily doses, I watched her closely, which reduced the knee dislocations. However, she always found something that needed her expert attention until Savannah experienced a real crisis, which lay just around the corner.

Dave, have you smelled this ear? I think it's infected.

SNIFF

Chapter 2 7

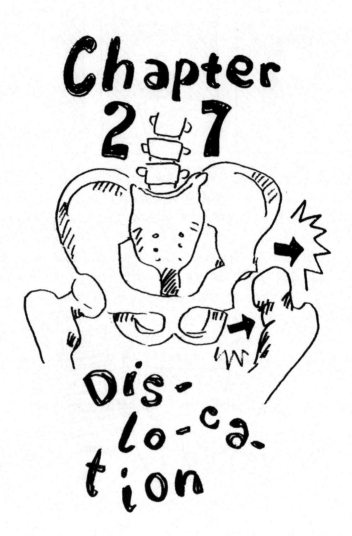

Dis-
lo-ca-
tion

2009

Radlology

WARN

When you get her settled, I'll help you with your lead smock.

The tech dressed me in the heavy suit.

When we were done, we looked like Samurai.

The radiologist appeared.

Make her lie straighter. I can't get a good picture. Let's try again.

Straighter? Does he not understand why we're here in the first place?

I know, right?

The tech appeared to be in her mid-twenties. Her tentative touch with Savannah let me know she didn't have her own kids. I wanted to ask her if the experience of seeing broken children day after day affected her own outlook regarding having children. She knew all the things that could go wrong. However, the question felt too personal, so I kept it to myself.

After x-ray, we returned to the waiting room.

How much of our life energy had we expended in this purgatory?

When would we be released from this cycle?

Savannah Borden) The medical industrial complex has no respect for time or discomfort. In fact, they use it to exert power over us.

Good people work in the system, such as the Samurai-Tech. But they are only cogs in a vast dehumanizing cash machine.

I read many chapter books to Savannah while waiting for doctors.

"Seaward ho! Hang the treasure! It's the glory of the sea that has turned my head."

Ironically, the waits for the bone doctors were the longest — the waiting put so much stress on her twisted body that she screamed with pain!

shh.

Wah!

We can put a man on the moon, but we can't figure out how to reduce the hours of waiting. It's a solvable problem that they don't wish to solve.

Wah!

Dr. Bone arrived with his entourage: an assistant, a nurse, a therapist, and a social worker.

Hello, doing well?

Fine

Let's get a look at your hip, Savannah.

It's okay I'm here.

I liked Dr. Bone. He was gentle and easy going. He talked to Savannah as if she were a person, which made me happy.

This might hurt a little.

Chapter 28

Spinal Fusion

We arrived early at the hospital for Savannah's spinal fusion surgery. The hospital minaret reminded me of Morocco.

Dr. Tinker told us we could fix-

her spine with rods and screws

She had grown so uncomfortable -with a 70° curvature. She struggled in any position

The nurse placed the I.V.

We watched cartoons

"When will that cat ever learn?"

The anesthesi- ologist came to tell us the dangers of anesthesia

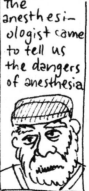

Dr. Tinker came to say hello.

Savannah smiled through pre-op. She enjoyed the attention of the doctors and nurses. She was so brave.

When they rolled her to the operating room, she laughed the whole way.

We were reunited in the Pediatric Intensive Care Unit, or PICU.

Tamara went to get a cup of water. I put on a sweatshirt I'd brought. Hospitals are cold places.

It took a while because I needed to help another mom find the water.

We overheard the nurses changing shifts.

These parents know what they're doing. This is not their first rodeo.

Ok.

Beep... Beep...

I picked up Ruby and we found a quiet room in which to eat take-out.

I have homework.

Is everything alright in here?

Yes. Thank you

What was that about?

I think this room is used for grieving families. They must think we're grieving.

The first night was my turn to keep vigil. I watched her sleep. She was so beautiful and peaceful in spite of everything.

The next day, they woke her up and removed the breathing tube.

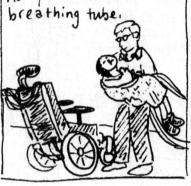

With the help of her physical therapist, we put her in her chair.

Wow! you look amazing!

you are so straight.

Savannah smiled at her straight body.

Once at home we were careful with her care. Nurse BM dove into the intensity of it.

Let's get you sponged down Ya-Ya.

After six weeks, Savannah had healed wonderfully. I took her for a check-up with Dr. Tinker. I donned the lead Samurai suit and we sat for a few x-ray portraits

click.

Chapter

29

Spinal
Illusion

I've watched this experience destroy people - the stress - the fatigue - the emotional and physical drain - the constant state of crisis.

How is it that I continue to rise?

Today... I will... I will survive... today.

I slept in our house alone. Tamara had taken first night shift at the hospital. Tomorrow would be my turn.

The PICU is so depressing. It drains you of time and energy.

We waited for them to withdraw sedation and wake her up. We drank coffee.

Beep...

When she was awake, we put her in her chair. The second time was more exhausting than triumphant.

She was happy to be up, but tired of the hospital, tired of being sliced and drugged.

sob

Not long after going home, Nurse BM pointed it out.

Do you see that orange spot? That's infection.

I immediately took her back to Dr. Tinker.

Definately infected.

moan.

She needs surgery. I'll have to open her back, clean it out, and install a wound vac. We'll culture the infection, so Dr. Germ can target an anti-biotic effectively.

A wound vac is a system that drains a wound while helping to pull the sides closed at the same time. It uses a block of foam-rubber inserted into the wound, attached to a pump by a hose.

Sponge inserted into her back.

Infecto Suk Inc.

The hum and gurgle of the wound vac was strangely soothing..

infuser

slush gurgle

wound vac

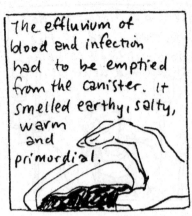

The effluvium of blood and infection had to be emptied from the canister. It smelled earthy, salty, warm and primordial.

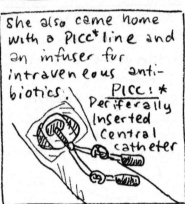

She also came home with a PICC* line and an infuser for intravenous antibiotics.

PICC: * Periferally Inserted Central Catheter

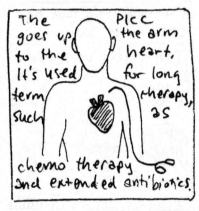

The PICC goes up the arm to the heart. It's used for long term therapy, such as chemo therapy and extended antibiotics.

The hospital sent two sales reps. to teach me how to use the antibiotic infuser:

This isn't the model we trained on

?

?

I figured out how to use the infuser and taught the reps, who were grateful.

Luckily, A nurse came to show me how to operate

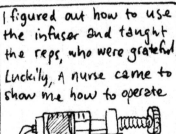

the PICC ... whew!

A few times, the plastic sheeting that covered the foam sprung a leak. I had to patch it with extra sheeting they gave me.

The antibiotics were so strong that Savannah developed very serious diarrhea.

oh you poor thing

I don't even know where to start.

She stayed out of school for months. Nurse BM got the extra hours she wanted, which made her happy.

As Savannah healed, the sponge in her back had to be downsized at the hospital...

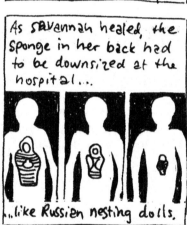

...like Russian nesting dolls.

At a routine appointment with Dr. Germ, Nurse BM resumed her old ways.

Dr. Germ, don't you think her face is infected? It's swollen here.

I'll look closer.

Hmm. Savannah, I'm going to tickle your face.

It's not an infection. Her face is lopsided.

No! Infection!

Weeks later, we returned to Dr. Germ on a day Nurse BM was off.

Her T-cells look good. How's the diahrrea?

Still terrible

I'm sorry.

I want to see if your cheek is still swollen. I'm going to tickle your neck.

It's not swollen. It's lopsided.

This is not infection. I think her face is like you say.

And our nurse makes these things up. She has Munchausen by Proxy.

If that's true. It's very serious.

We've tried to catch her but she's too clever. We've tried to replace her, but it's hard to find a nurse that wants our hours.

We can't change right now. It's not a good time... not with her out of school like this... We can't afford to miss that much work.

It's never a good time for difficult change.

Good luck to you both.

gag

Never a good time? It's really about having the will to change.

Chapter 30

The Communication Device

Imagine a child, locked in silence, strapped into a wheel chair because she can't walk or even hold her head up.

Now, imagine it's your child and she's ten years old

She's never said "Hi." or "I love you." And she never will. Her brain injury prevents her.

giggle

One day you visit her at school. She clicks a button and says:

Hello. *click* !

Hello, Savannah.

Hello.

click

giggle

It's the most amazing word you've ever heard.

Hello. Hello. Hello.

giggle

click

Hello.

After the visit, I couldn't help but smile all the way back to my car.

Suddenly, I couldn't hold it together any longer.

NON-VERBAL MY ASS!

I wept tears of joy. I'd always known she was in there.

Much later, when Nurse BM learned about the communication device, she got self-righteous.

Why don't you use it at home?

We have. We choose to give her a break at home.

I think you should use it.

It's not that simple. She's still learning. As part of the training you MUST honor every request.

That doesn't sound bad.

She has a wicked sense of humor.

Savannah healed enough to start back to school after missing nearly the whole year.

Wah!

She came home crying every day.

Why are you so upset, Ya-ya?

Wah

She was still crying when I got home from work.

weh!

what's going on?

We tried changing positions, changing TV shows, pain medication. Nothing helped.

Savannah, what are you trying to tell me? I want to understand.

One day, Nurse BM was out sick and I had to meet Savannah's bus.

giggle

We laughed and watched TV all evening.

giggle giggle

I love this show, too.

giggle giggle

Next day...

wah!

and the next...

wah!

I think something is seriously wrong with her.

There's something seriously wrong with you...

Maybe.

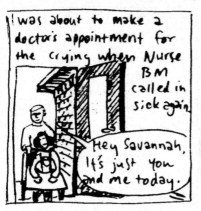

I was about to make a doctor's appointment for the crying when Nurse BM called in sick again.

Hey Savannah, it's just you and me today.

Savannah didn't cry. In fact, we had a great evening.

giggle

Later that night.

Have you noticed that Savannah doesn't cry when I meet the bus?

I think we have to consider that Savannah may be trying to tell us something loud and clear.

She's trying to tell us that she doesn't want Nurse BM.

Oh my God, you're right.

It all makes sense. Doesn't it?

If Savannah's done - I'm done.

Me, too.

It'll be hard to go without a nurse until we find a new one.

We'll have to take on the hardship - if it makes Savannah happy...

...that's all that matters.

"Take her home and love her" had become "make her happy."

I'll call the agency tomorrow

Once again, it was just us. It's never a good time for change

But it's always the right time to do the right thing.

Chapter
31

Removing the
Training Wheels

When Ruby was seven, she asked me to remove her training wheels...

...because she wanted to participate in the Annual Rosedale Ride,

...a fundraising event for Savannah's school.

Money from the event goes to buy equipment, such as Savannah's communication device.

Ruby had unsuccessfully tried to ride without training wheels for a week.

Daddy!

Let's try again.

We had one day left.

Before the Rosedale Ride, the local TV station interviewed Tamara and Savannah.

"Rosedale saved our lives."

Savannah grew bored.

"Let's blow this popsicle stand!"

click

Ha Ha Ha Ha

Ha giggle Ha giggle Ha

Ruby and I lined up for the kid's Ride

"Daddy, can you give me a push."

"Ride, Ride, Ride, Ride your bike!"

"Any time"

"Hey, Sister!"

It was as if I had woken up from a long sleep - ten years - ten years lost in a fog - but here was life, still streaming. I didn't want to miss any of these sparkling moments. I removed my own training wheels and tried life again.

223

Chapter 32

The Courage to Rise

Though strangers to me — I didn't feel that I was a stranger to them.

I knew a young couple once... full of energy and optimism...

...who found the courage to rise in the darkness... We'll get through this together.

...and found gratitude for what they had.

Ha Ha Ha Ha Ha Ha Ha Ha Ha Ha

Come on, Savannah, let's go home.

Chapter 33

A Happy Halloween

229

Trick or treaters swarmed past. A woman pulled a wagon with a baby and a beer cooler.

Ruby and Nurse V. kept going as we stopped to refill our cups.

I'm glad Nurse V. brought Savannah out tonight.

Me, too. This has been a lot of fun.

I never thought we'd trick-or-treat as a family.

I thought this was one of those things we'd have to give up.

It feels strange to be happy.

It's as if we've returned from a really long, really bad trip.

Savannah wants to go in and have her bath.

Good night. I'm so glad you came out with us tonight.

giggle giggle giggle

Good night, Savannah. See you in the morning.

giggle Ha! Ha!

Thank you for bringing her out tonight.

No problem.

We'd given up on stuff like this.

Glad to help. Y'all deserve it after what you've been through.

The Second Chance Prom

Chapter 34

FLASHBACK TO 2011: Rosedale PTA breakfast meeting...

I've come to grips with the fact that my son will never drive a car or have a date.

...or get married and have children.

...Or go to prom.

Oh, Prom. All the angst and joy! Who do you ask, and the dress - like a brides'maid you think it's good, but it's not. Every bride promises you can wear it again.

And the hair! I was a brides'maid in Dallas - you should've seen my hair and make-up!

You know, I'll never see Savannah get married. I can't control that... but Prom...

Oh my gosh, Tamara, that's it! We can put on a Prom. A "second-chance" Prom - It's as much for the parents as the kids.

"Who should get to go?"

"Everyone. Let's be real— we don't know who'll be here year to year."

"What's the worst that can happen? Savannah gets to go to many Proms."

2012

The idea was so powerful that the staff and a group of parents made it happen.

ROSEDALE PROM

They decorated the whole school.

giggle

"You look like you're going to Prom... maybe because you are!"

You look gorgeous!

I love what you've done with your hair.

Strolling the halls was like walking the red carpet of paparazzi.

Savannah had to eat, so I turned on her pump in the "chill" room.

We headed to the cafeteria for a father-daughter dance.

Ruby wanted one, too. Tamara took Savannah for a spin.

Daddy, more! more!

Let's check on Savannah.

She had finished eating and needed a diaper change. We took her to her classroom.

I bet you never thought you'd be changing a diaper at Prom?

There are a lot of things I didn't think I'd be doing.

Heading back to the party, we passed the wall of Remembrance, where photos of children who passed away while students are displayed.

People packed the cafeteria: teachers, parents, and students. Everyone was laughing and smiling. People danced together, alone, and in groups. A few parents had plucked their kids from their wheelchairs and danced with them in their arms.

It's getting late - we should pack up to go.

But as we were leaving

"I will Survive" by Gloria Gaynor started playing.

Wait.

Tamara stopped in her tracks.

We can't miss this.

Ruby, watch your sister.

These people, long hidden in the margins

Suddenly came alive—so joyful, so beautiful

Savannah had broken us down and rebuilt us with the courage and will to believe in the future.

All the Moms screamed

I will Survive I will Survive Hey! Hey!

Chapter 35
The Art
of Being
Savannah

I've been living all wrong... Life isn't about career goals and increasing assets and treating time as a commodity.

Maybe life is about something else, entirely?

I love your hair

Savannah didn't want what others had

She loved her friends and family fearlessly.

Do you want to watch "Glee" with me?

I love this episode — you know, the one where...

giggle giggle

If any one is going to reach Nirvana, it's going to be Savannah.

She found happiness in the simplest things:

holding hands,

going for a walk

Sharing music with Nurse C.

Edelweiss
Edelweiss

She lived her life in each moment

Time for your bath.

She didn't mean to teach us anything, but she taught us so much...

Courage and grace, she taught us that the voiceless can have the most to say if we will only make the effort to listen.

When she'd had enough of this world, she left us abruptly — like a book that ends just as it was getting good.

The truth is horrific and beautiful...

...and yet we rise

A Final Thought:

The Truth is Horrific and Beautiful

"When you embrace your child, or your brother, or your friend... remind yourself that you love someone who is mortal; that you love what is not yours to own. These people are allowed you only for the present, not irrevocably, nor forever; but as a fig, or a bunch of grapes, in the appointed season... What harm is there, while you kiss your child, in saying to yourself, 'To-morrow you may die;' and to say to your friend, 'To-morrow we may part, and we may never see each other again?'"

Epictetus, The Discourses, Book 3

We are here for the briefest of moments, so we must cherish what we have and remember that tomorrow it could all be gone... even those whom we love the most. This truth is horrific becuase it asks us to face our mortality. However, it is beautiful becuase it liberates us from the tyranny of dread.

With this memoir, I hoped to show you that this life can be hard and ugly, but we should not shy away from those realities. To deny them is to increase their power over us. To embrace the mistakes, the failures, the heartbreak, the tragedy without glorifying it, is to live in a way that allows us to fully engage with the world. Savannah made us see life as a beautiful sandpainting, a fig tree, a smile that could melt your heart. She challenged us, and now she challenges you to be fully present, and to live with empathy, compassion, and love.

David Borden
Austin, Texas
March 2017

About the Author & Illustrator

David Borden is an artist and award winning writer living in Austin, Texas with his wife and daughter. He's held various jobs in education: director of art programming at a non-profit for persons with disabilities, ESL and GED instructor, and college administrator. Once, long ago, he even sold everything and moved to Morocco for five years. He is often described as unconventional, irreverent, and indomitable. His oldest daughter taught him to laugh loudly, face every day with courage, and dare to dream.

Other Books by David Borden

Make America Purr Again:
Cat Wisdom on How to Heal the Divisions
between Human Americans

ISBN: 978-1-36-648972-2

Acknowlgement to Genius:

Acknowledgements

Charlotte Gullick for helping me to see the potential of this project. Tamara Atkinson for supporting me in the many, many hours spent writing and drawing. Ruby for her critical eye and undying love. Elizabeth Dickey for being the most awesome principal at the most awesome school: Rosedale. Savannah's many wonderful teachers and therapists. The Rosedale PTA. Charlene Gill, my greatest editor and encourager. Drs. Terwelp, Holt, Busse, and Bryant... if only all doctors could be as caring, engaged, and competent. Nathan Livni who's brilliant insights always challenged me to write better. Austin Community College and Mike Midgley for being flexible and understanding. Dreux Carpenter who never ceased to pump up my ego over drafts of the project and draughts of beer. My parents for taking care of Savannah overnight in the early years. Jessica Vess for her marketing experise. The many wonderful and generous backers from Kickstarter. All my beta readers: Beverly Veltman (eternal love and thanks), Angie Mills, Linda Welsh, Kathy Dowdy, Zac, Kim Goss, and Janelle Blank. Sarah Byrd and Chris Purkiss, who are the amazing friends in good times and bad.

I'd also like to thank Austin Public Libraries for keeping me in graphic novels and reference materials, Pacha and Flightpath cafes for keeping me in tea and inspiring workspaces, Malvern Books for hosting the Lion and Pirate Open Mike for VSA Texas and Coalition of Texans with Disabilities (Pen 2 Paper) and for giving a voice to brave people, Open Door Preschools for being there in our greatest time of need, the UT Cowboys for their volunteerism and fundraising efforts, especially Bernardo who took Savannah to the prom and made her so happy, and The Rosedale Foundation for raising the money that gave Savannah a voice.

CPSIA information can be obtained
at www.ICGtesting.com
Printed in the USA
LVOW01s1026010417
529286LV00008B/240/P